Charlest

Richard and Bridg

Tor Mark • Redruth

For further information of all the titles in this series please visit:-
www.tormark.co.uk

First published 1994
Second edition 2006
This reprint 2010

Tor Mark Press, United Downs Ind Est, St Day, Redruth, Cornwall TR16 5HY

Printed by R Booth Ltd, The Praze, Penryn, Cornwall TR10 8AA

ISBN 978 085025 350 4

Front cover: Square Sail ships inner dock 1992.
Back cover: Square Sail ships inner dock 1992 with one of the last coasters loading china clay

Title page: Aerial view of Charlestown 1978

Reverse title page: The early steam driven Foden lorries were replaced in the 1930s by these smaller petrol driven vehicles. This fleet is shown lined up outside the Pier House Hotel c 1936

Acknowledgements
The photographs are reproduced by kind permission of the following:-
Charlestown Estate Ltd – pages 4, 10, 11, 15(top), 21(top), 24, 25, 26, 31(lower): ECC plc – 2 & 13: Arthur Hosegood – 27(top): Richard Larn – 3, 8, 9, 15(lower), 18, 19, 20(both), 28, 29, 31(top), 32 and both covers: Roger Parker – 1 & 30: Veronica Rashleigh, Menabilly Estate – 6: Royal Institution of Cornwall – 12, 14, 21(lower), 22, 23, 27 (lower): J C Burrow – centre pages

A brief history of the port

Scenes like this, with men and women alike helping to unload a ship's cargo in an attempt to 'beat the tide', when work would have to cease for six hours, were still common all around Cornwall in the eighteenth and nineteenth centuries. The hazard to small ketches and luggers such as these was considerable, since if the wind increased and shifted to blow on-shore, they were liable to be wrecked.

Polmear Cove, in which the port of Charlestown is situated, was used to beach small craft in just this way. It was also sometimes known as Porthmear. 'Mear' means large, 'pol' means a pool or deep water anchorage and 'porth' suggests sand on which boats could be beached.

As the mines and china clay pits in the St Austell area flourished in the late eighteenth century, the need for a local port with security from the weather, deep water and proper unloading facilities became obvious to the local entrepreneur Charles Rashleigh, after whom the port is named.

ST. BLAZE

PORTH

Black Rock
Spit Point
MERTHES
Foxmire Pt.
Bream Rk.
Killgevaders Bank
Shortharna Pt.
Shortharna Peak
Triania Pt.
Sandy Rock Toun
A Gull Pt.
CRINNIS
Appletree Toun
POLMEAR
Landrine Rock
Bier
Polmear Jd.
The Battery
DUPORTH
Carrack Owd Point
Carrack Owd Rock
Cargiavy Point
LOWER PORTHPEAN
HIGHER PORTHPEAN
Sand Drage Rock
Flat Rock Point
Silver mine Point
Gwendra Point

ST. AUSTELL PARISH

GOTTAM TOWER R
Val d'Ebor
Puckeys R
The Elbow
Polmear R
Duporth R
The Melon Rough

Some eighty percent of the buildings visible in the aerial photograph on the title page, taken in 1978, were built in the period 1791-1800. It was a planned village, and the plan was rapidly executed, which accounts for its coherent overall character. Charlestown makes no pretensions to quaintness or higgledy-piggledy prettiness, but is a genuine working port.

In 1790 the population was just nine fishermen and their families. Charles Rashleigh began building a pier for fishing boats in 1791; the inner basin (or dock) and its associated industries rapidly followed. A great deal of the hillside had to be cut away to create the port, and it was all done by hand. The job was virtually complete in ten years.

A supply of water was necessary to sustain the depth in the dock; at high tide the dock gate is shut, holding back most of the water, but some leakage around the gates is inevitable.

There was no suitable local supply, and Rashleigh had to build a leat all the way from Luxulyan, four miles inland - 'an expensive and tortuous watercourse' according to Polsue, author of *Lake's Parochial History of Cornwall*, in 1867. He goes on to say: 'From this time its rise was rapid. It soon had a good hotel, shipwright's yard and a rope manufactury, and several pilchard seans established, and the basin was enlarged sufficiently to receive vessels of more than 200 tons. On the cliff to the side of the harbour a battery was erected. Charlestown has now [1867] a large and respectable population, a church, a Wesleyan chapel, an iron foundry and a smelting house for tin. Large quantities of china clay and stone, and copper ores are shipped.'

The population was large, probably around three thousand by the time Polsue wrote, but whether it was quite as respectable as he claims may be doubted. It was after all a port with visiting sailors; another writer, in 1834, 'was much impressed with the scenes of idleness, dissipation and immorality I witnessed. The labourers and mechanics neglecting their work, not only losing their ordinary wages but spending the money required for the support of their families at beer shops and keil [bowling] alleys. The sailor staggering home drunk, using the most horrid oaths is an object of terror and pity to all reflecting persons.' Sailors were also catered for at the houses of ill repute known to this day as 'Eleven Doors'.

St Austell Bay was known as Tywardreath Bay until the late eighteenth century, and the chart (opposite) is believed to date from around 1794, when Polmear was in its infancy. The prominent gun battery was built in 1793. A battery was necessary for all ports during the Napoleonic wars, both as a deterrent to invasion and to prevent destructive raids against shipping. It was maintained until 1898 and manned for practice shooting by the Crinnis Cliff Volunteers, later renamed the Cornwall Artillery Volunteers.

The founder of Charlestown was Charles Rashleigh (1747-1823) who gave his name to the port. The Rashleigh family came from Fowey, where they and the Treffrys had long vied with each other for influence in the town, the Rashleighs being Whig and the Treffrys Tory. Charles was born at Menabilly Manor (later to be the temporary home of Daphne du Maurier). He qualified early as an attorney-at-law and became Town Clerk of St Austell and Grampound and Recorder for Fowey, Wadebridge and other courts. He was also Deputy Sheriff of Cornwall and Land Agent for the Duchies of Cornwall and Lancaster. In addition he owned and ran two legal practices, a bank, a tin-smelting business and a number of other concerns.

He married Grace Tremayne of Heligan, who bore him three daughters. Unfortunately his career was blighted by his misguided trust in rogue servants; one such episode caused him a loss equivalent to nearly £10,000,000 in today's currency, and another his manor house.

One of these rogue servants was Joseph Dingle, who lived at Polmear Farm. He was associated with Charles Rashleigh for almost 45 years, having been taken out of the St Austell workhouse as a boy of twelve and apprenticed to a carpenter. At the age of 22, he appears on the staff records of Duporth House, Rashleigh's manor, as his servant and footman, and was later to become Superintendent of Works for the construction of the port of Charlestown. From 1790 onward, the year in which construction began, Dingle deliberately withheld rents, dock-money and port dues from his employer, systematically stealing at least £25,000 by 1805, before Rashleigh recognised the wholesale theft which was going on. By 1811, when the case reached court, the sum had risen to an estimated £32,000, an absolute fortune in those days. Dingle was bankrupted after protracted legal proceedings and died a pauper in receipt of parish support. The loss of such a large sum also contributed to Rashleigh's own financial downfall, and he was to die bankrupt and almost penniless in 1823.

When Duporth Manor was to be sold, shortly after Charles Rashleigh's death, it was the subject of a strange incident. A certain Dr Bull of Bristol was the very first person arrested by police as a result of information transmitted to them by telegraph; this concerned the murder of a girl in London, whom Dr Bull had 'misled'. Only a week or so earlier Dr Bull and a friend had come down to St Austell pretending they wanted to buy Duporth Manor; they asked to see the title deeds and the solicitor left them alone in a room to study them. It was later found that they had walked out, and the documents were never seen again. The property was later sold to a Mr Freeth, without the deeds ever being found.

It is hard looking at the quiet scene in the dock today to realise just how busy this little port was, but scenes like this one in 1914 were not uncommon. A tramway ran along the top of the dock on the eastern side, and china clay from the trucks, called 'trams', could be tipped straight down the chutes into the hold of the ship, in this case the SS *Westdale*.

It was said to be possible on almost any day of the week to walk from one side of the dock to the other by stepping from deck to deck, sometimes four abreast. The complex task of supervising the movement of vessels within the dock once the gates were closed, and their unloading and loading, was in the nineteenth century the responsibility of the Dockmaster. The Harbour Master at that time was responsible for pilotage, opening and closing the dock gates and getting the vessels in and out. Every high tide, day and night, saw the gates open and vessels entering or leaving.

For 25 years Charlestown was the only port between Fowey and Mevagissey, but then Pentewan was built in 1826 and Par a few years later. Pentewan had a railway link to St Austell. By that time Rashleigh was dead, or perhaps he would have built a line too. Then Par was built as an artificial harbour on a much grander scale by J T Austen, who changed his name to Treffry. He owned a substantial number of the mines inland, and built a railway to connect them to his new port. Such competition might have crippled Charlestown, but the fantastic growth of the china clay industry between 1830 and 1914, and then the demise of Pentewan through silting, meant that it went instead from strength to strength.

But Charlestown had been designed for small sailing ships, and cargo vessels were growing ever larger. Unlike its rivals, it had a dock: vessels did not have to beach themselves at low tide which was a great advantage, but the dock entrance had to be narrow enough to be closed by wooden gates. In 1971 the entrance to the dock was widened and improved, with a new folding gate replacing the old wooden gates so that coasters up to 600 tons could now enter to load china clay (there were no longer imports, as there used to be, of coal, timber and fertilizers) but it was a tight squeeze to get such vessels in, as this photograph of the *Magda Wegener* of Hamburg shows; there is probably no more than eight inches clearance on either side, and only three feet beneath her keel.

The advantage of Charlestown was its proximity to the china clay works beyond St Austell, and the fact that ships could be quickly loaded, arriving on one tide and sailing on the next; but the older generation of 500 ton coasters was slowly replaced with modern vessels far too large to enter the port. The very last clay shipment from Charlestown was the MV *Ellen* on 13 December 1999.

The industries of Charlestown

In the outer basin, seen here from the western pier, a fleet of seine boats was moored in constant readiness during the summer months, in case a shoal of pilchards or mackerel was sighted close inshore. One of the locals, the 'huer' or look-out man, stood high up in the gun battery or on Crinnis Cliffs. His job was to alert the village if he spotted a shoal, then to guide the boats once they had put to sea.

It was always a mad scramble to man the seine boats and lurkers, everyone dropping whatever they had been doing to get out to the shoal and surround it by 'shooting' the nets, stopping the fish from moving on. Catches were often phenomenal, as many as a million pilchards being caught at one time, but this was not a daily occurrence: a whole season could sometimes pass without one shoal, and overfishing was diminishing the fish stocks from 1880 onwards.

Whenever a catch was made, women were employed in large numbers in the pilchard cellars of Charlestown, gutting and cleaning the fish and 'bulking' them in layers of salt to allow the natural juices to drain, before packing them in more salt for export to the Catholic countries of Europe. When a cask was full, the fish were put under pressure using an iron screw-jack which forced out much of the oil before the lid of the barrel was secured.

The port once had three such cellars, each an independent business, which were named *Content*, *Rashleigh* and *Friends' Endeavour*, each employing a dozen people. The men caught the fish and brought them ashore, with the children helping to carry them from the beach to the cellars.

From 1792 until 1875 when the size of the inner dock was increased, its north end was used for shipbuilding using a long earth and stone ramp which held three slipways side by side. The ramp also accommodated various shipwrights, workshops, timber stores and a smithy. Over 30 ships of different sizes were built here, some of 500 tons; they were launched into the dock before being fitted out. This photograph, taken from the battery field on the western side of the dock, shows a small craft being repaired at the top of the ramp whilst a vessel of some size is under construction on the slipway itself.

The last ship to be built at Charlestown, the schooner *Flying Spray*, was constructed and launched by John Stephens on the western beach, but not without problems. In the attempt to get her afloat, the support props collapsed and she lay on her side until the next high tide when she was successfully righted.

Whilst fishing and shipbuilding were important industries, it was the mining industry which justified the expense of building the dock at Charlestown. Although little remains now except a number of collapsed or partially covered mine shafts, a few adits and heaps of spoil, the area around the village once contained a vast tin and copper mining industry. In the eighteenth and early nineteenth century Polgooth Mine was one of the leading tin mines in Cornwall and by 1864 Charlestown United Ltd employed over 500 people; there were three blowing or smelting houses in St Austell, producing 4137 blocks of tin in 1824, and even two blowing houses within the village, which boasted its own assay office.

From the early 1800s for almost seventy years vast quantities of copper ore were taken from the Crinnis mines - 10,000 tons in 1814 alone, although only six years earlier an expert had declared them 'not worth a pipe of tobacco'.

But the industry which came to dominate Charlestown was china clay. Clay was moved from the 'dries' through the streets of St Austell and Mount Charles down to the port of Charlestown in horse-drawn carts. The photograph (left) shows Bert Grose driving the very last horse-drawn load in July 1949. Never less than two and sometimes four horses were needed to pull the five-ton loads up and down the steep hills.

The approach to the port, then known as the Great Charlestown Road, was and still is the widest approach to any town or village in Cornwall. Before pavements were introduced, it was sufficiently wide for six carts to be abreast at a time, a measure of the importance of the trade and the foresight of Charles Rashleigh. It was unmade and rough surfaced until 1912 and the iron 'drags' - portable brakes attached to the wheels when going downhill - tore great grooves in the road and created dust.

Dust came also from the clay itself. When it was unloaded at the dockside, even a slight wind would cover the whole village in a thin film of white clay. Lumps of clay fell from the carts as they jolted their way from St Austell so that the entire route from the clay pits to the ship, and the people and houses along the route, were all severely contaminated.

Much of the clay was loaded into the holds of the ships down overhead chutes, but it was often necessary for the driver to shovel the dried lumps known as 'ball clay', one man regularly moving twenty tons a day. This scene shows an early steamship, with open bridge and wheel, taking on a cargo of clay by hand.

This is the Lower Charlestown clay dry, shortly after it was built by Messrs Lovering in 1906, one of two constructed in the village at the turn of the century. This one still stands, close to the dock; the other has been demolished, but stood near Denver Engineering's Charlestown Foundry. The clay was pumped to the works in slurry form from Carclaze. A tipping 'tram' was wheeled onto a gantry, which was rolled from one end of the building to the other, pouring the slurry evenly across the floor or 'pan'. Coal-fired underfloor heating gradually dried the clay until it was stiff enough to be cut into blocks, which were then shovelled out and down into the lin-hay, on the left in this picture.

The clay was there loaded into trams, each carrying about half a ton. They were pushed by hand from the dry and along a covered gallery cantilevered out over the dock; then the clay was tipped down chutes directly into the hold (above, right).

Later, clay was transported to Charlestown by covered lorries, carrying fifteen to twenty tons each. The chutes are much the same (below, right).

Charlestown Dock was taken over by the Admiralty in WW 11 and used for the outfitting of Royal Navy wooden motor vessels (MFVs) which were generally used by the navy throughout the fleet as tenders. Later, Curtis of Totnes, shipbuilders, established a yard at Par, building 38 wooden motor mine

sweepers known as MMSs. They were towed to Charlestown to have their machinery fitted and generally finished. Their crews of 21 officers and ratings joined the ships in the port and sailed straight to war after trials.

A walk round the village

Visitors wanting to explore the village fully are advised to start on the road from St Austell, just above Church Lane (the church dates from 1851) at the old Charlestown Foundry and Ironworks, started in 1823 by James Thomas, and one of the first in the West Country to work from blueprints. They produced mining machinery (including a beam engine for Mexico, no single part of which was heavier than one mule could carry) as well as shovels, kibbles, chains and any other component which was required. After the decline in mining, the foundry turned to the china clay industry, and later changed hands several times before being sold for development in 2004. Until 1880 the tilt hammers were steam operated, but then were replaced by smaller ones driven by this water wheel.

The leat which served the dock crossed the road no less than four times, so that water could be diverted by sluices for different functions. There was a water wheal attached to Mill House; another drove the china clay crushing plant in the yard behind a fine two-storied granite building with stone steps to the top floor. Water also worked the bellows for the blowing house. So important was the leat that the Charlestown Estate once employed a full-time leat man, who did nothing other than clear weed and maintain the banks, sluices and reservoir ponds all the way back to the Luxulyan valley. The village blacksmith's shop can be seen on the west side of the road, just above Church Lane, with a letterbox in the end wall.

The picture below is of the 'Eleven Doors' which lay derelict for many years prior to development at the end of the C20th. This was a part of a collection of farm buildings which ended with the front doors of eleven cottages facing into a small lane. Also known as 'China Town', it developed something of a reputation in the late Victorian period when it was frequented by visiting seamen seeking and presumably finding ladies of easy virtue.

The large granite building in the foreground, once a barn and later a china-stone crushing plant, has been a store, piano factory, dancing school, bicycle repair shop and is now the offices and workshop of Partech Electronics Ltd, an internationally famous company specialising in the design and manufacture of water quality instrumentation.

Farms were worked in the village even after the port was constructed. One, un-named until the late 1800s when it was called West Polmear Farm, (top photo), is now subdivided into four private houses. Polmear Farm, which was so named even before the port was constructed, is still a working farm, located only yards from the dock; its buildings stand immediately in front of the huge clay-dry with its chimney dominating the skyline. It was once occupied by the infamous Joseph Dingle (see page 7).

Wooden casks or barrels were used in the old days for a great many commodities, not just for beer, and in Charlestown there were three cooperages employing up to forty men: Rouse's cooperage survived until the late 1940s. They made casks for salted pilchards, large casks like these for high quality china clay, and more substantial 'wet' barrels for beer, salt meat and vinegar. The lower picture shows the casks being filled with clay, a job which created endless clouds of dust and was one of the worst in the industry.

Scenes from Charlestown's past

Incoming vessels unloaded on the west side of the dock (on the right looking towards the sea) and were then moved to the east side for loading. Since many boats brought coal, it was not unusual for the labourers to go home at midday black with coal dust after a morning on the west side, and in the evening white with clay dust after an afternoon on the east side.

Here Baltic timber staves for the cooperages are being unloaded from a coaster into Norman May's fleet of Commer lorries, around 1935. In the background can be seen the mast and furled sail of a spritsail barge, probably from Plymouth, with another sailing vessel ahead of the coaster. The use of barrels for transporting clay ceased in the late 1940s, when larger diesel tipping lorries were introduced for bulk carriage, and ships accepted loose bulk china clay in their holds.

The photograph opposite was probably taken in 1914, when sail still predominated. The job of the dockmaster must have been a nightmare on days like this when there was scarcely a spare berth in the dock.

Looking down on the dock from the path leading to the battery, around 1890 (above) and around 1910 (right). The houses and cottages were built as part of the development of the port after 1791, but one building predates them, the *Content* pilchard cellar which faces the sea, with a lean-to veranda. This was the very first building erected, when Polmear Cove was just an inlet from which a handful of fishermen worked their boats, and probably dates from 1740. There were four dwellings above the cellar.

The large white building on the far right of the photograph was a huge limekiln; limestone was burnt as part of its preparation for dressing acid farmland soil. A pile of limestone or fuel lies outside, and the two piles of casks are probably the finished product awaiting shipment. The small vessel alongside is probably loading burnt lime, whilst inside the dock itself other craft are discharging coal or timber and taking on china clay. Charlestown had no less than seven lime-burning hearths, four of which today form part of the village pottery shop.

In addition to its main function, the limekiln was offering the public 'warm and cold seawater baths' in 1833, using the surplus heat from the burning limestone to heat water.

Here we have much the same viewpoint as that on the preceding page, but rather later, probably about 1910. The former *Content* fish cellar has lost its veranda. Today it is still possible to see in the seaward wall of this building the shaped granite holes through which wooden poles were placed which, over two centuries, wore away the upper surface of the stonework. These poles acted as levers; the pilchards in their casks inside the cellar were 'pressed' by forcing up the outer end of the pole with props. The harbour lime kiln has been pulled down, and replaced by the Harbourmaster's Round House, erected around 1900. One hearth of the limekiln still survives.

Gas lighting has been installed on the pier and dock area, but not before time: a number of seamen, including ships' masters, had lost their lives by falling into the dock at night and drowning, leading to severe criticism of the owners, Messrs Crowder, Sartoris & Co. The fact that most of the victims were returning from the Rashleigh Arms may have been a contributory factor.

The approach to the port faces south-east. When a south-east wind blows stronger than force 3 or 4 it becomes impossible to open the gates so ships inside find themselves unable to leave, and arrivals have to anchor outside or seek another port until the weather changes.

This photograph was taken in the summer of 1890, the year in which the wooden dock gates were renewed for the first time. (The new pair lasted until 1971.) In the centre stands what is now the Pier House Hotel, originally the Charlestown Hotel built in 1793; it became a farmhouse after the Rashleigh Arms was built. Then the occupants of the farm started taking in paying guests as farming prosperity declined before the 1914-18 War, until the farm once again became a hotel. The long building on the left was a malt-house, demolished in 1895 after a storm damaged the quay below it and undermined the building.

Where blocks of clay went straight from the Charlestown dries into the linhay, and thence to the ships, they had minimum handling and did not pick up much dirt. However, clay transported by cart from any distance often picked up dirt, gravel or sand and had to be cleaned. This was done by 'bal-maidens', girls and women who scraped the blocks to remove any contaminating dirt and maintain the purity of the product. In this photograph (below right) from around 1900 the dirty blocks are to the left, the clean blocks neatly stacked to the right.

Well dressed spectators, suggesting that it was probably a Sunday or public holiday, possibly even Regatta Monday, watch the arrival of the very first steamship to enter the port, the SS *Iron Duke*, bringing in coal about 1890. Presumably it is the harbour pilot at the ship's wheel, standing behind the vertical boiler which protrudes up through the deck, whilst a sailor stands on the 'turtle-back' forecastle holding a mooring rope, in front of a rolled-up foresail.

The unique and relatively unchanged character of the village and port has attracted numerous film-makers. Opposite a sailing ship depicting the *Beagle* is part of a film-set for *Darwin's Voyage of Discovery*, telling the story of the five year voyage which provided Darwin with the clues to deduce his theory of evolution. Other films have included *The Eagle has Landed*, *The Day of the Triffids*, *The Three Musketeers*, *Moll Flanders*, *A Respectable Trade*, *The Odyssey*, *Amazing Grace*, *African Squadron*, *Pandemonium*, *Man to Man* and *The New World*.

Historic films require historic extras and Charlestown has never been short of the necessary manpower. Here a group of ten men await their call, on temporary seating outside what was once the *Rashleigh* pilchard cellar on the west side of the dock.

The Charlestown Cliff Rescue Volunteers, with breeches buoy apparatus cart in the background, around 1910. Charlestown had its own coastguard unit at the time, with a station officer and four coastguards, who were in fact serving members of the Royal Navy. The white armbands were the volunteer's badge of office, issued when they attended an emergency or a practice; without it they would not get paid. The group is standing in front of the Pier House.

Above right: the ill-fated *Marques*, once a frequent visitor to Charlestown. Here she is rigged as a brig, preparing in the dock for what was to be her last voyage. Whilst engaged in a sail training cruise off the West Indies, she was caught in a squall, capsized and sank with the loss of 20 lives in 1984. One of Charlestown's attractions today is the superb Shipwreck and Heritage Centre, containing fascinating items brought up from the seabed, together with many historic photographs and galleries of local social history and the development of the port.

Below right: the entrance to the dock from seaward, photographed in late Victorian times. The Land Agent of the Estate is standing in the centre with his top hat and dog, with probably the Harbour Master to the left of him. On either side stand dock porters, the labourers who unloaded and loaded the ships and manned the capstans which opened the gates. The Charlestown of those days was a noisy bustling place, full of industrial activity, very unlike the village of today.

The start of another chapter in Charlestown's history. The three-masted wooden barque *Kaskelot* (Danish for 'sperm whale') enters her new home port on 26 March 1994. Launched in 1948, she has been used in many films and is owned by Square Sail Ltd, who now own the dock at Charlestown and use it as a permanent base for their many sailing ships.